ALBERTA

Text
Victoria J. Hutton

Captions
Fleur Robertson

Photography
Miller Comstock, Inc
Colour Library Books Ltd

Design
Teddy Hartshorn

Commissioning Editor
Andrew Preston

Publishing Assistant
Edward Doling

Editorial
David Gibbon
Gill Waugh

Production
Ruth Arthur
Sally Connolly
David Proffit
Andrew Whitelaw

Director of Production
Gerald Hughes

Director of Publishing
David Gibbon

CLB 2559
©1990 Colour Library Books Ltd, Godalming, Surrey, England.
All rights reserved.
This edition published 1990 by Bramley Books.
Colour separations by Advance Laser Graphic Arts, Hong Kong.
Printed and bound in Italy.
ISBN 0 86283 817 7

ALBERTA

VICTORIA J. HUTTON

Bramley Books

Tough, tenacious, yet possessed of an exquisite beauty, the wild rose of Alberta has come to embody this land's western spirit. To understand Alberta, one must look beyond the vastness of the mountain, plain and forest to consider the spirit that has attracted and sustained life for countless ages. It not only provided the source of the Indian peoples' rich native culture, but it later instilled courage in the early explorers and gave inspiration and strength to the settlers who followed. And like the wild rose, Alberta continues to flower and flourish within the extremes of nature, exhibiting extraordinary growth in its short history.

Alberta occupies a unique situation within Canada: set within 661,185 square kilometres (225,285 square miles) of breathtaking western landscape, the province combines a pristine patchwork of farmland in its centre with borders of dense forests to the north, grasslands to the south and the ancient slopes of the Rocky Mountains to the west.

It is the glacial rivers cascading down from the Rockies that have carved the province of Alberta into its natural geological divisions. In the north the Peace River leads the farmland deep into the boreal forest; the North Saskatchewan and its tributaries cut through the plains where wheat and grain-fed beef abound; in the south the Oldman and the Bow rivers flow together to become the South Saskatchewan, meandering through ancient Indian lands.

Alberta's northerly latitude keeps the province within the northern cool-temperate zone, yet this has not stopped the province from being known as Canada's sunniest. Its relatively high altitude and the clear air make for week upon week of bright, sunny days and clear, starry nights. A phenomenon of the climate is the strange chinook wind that characterizes a winter in Alberta. These are warm, dry winds that funnel through the Rockies, particularly in southwestern Alberta, raising the freezing temperatures dramatically within hours, melting snow and exposing the grass, providing a warm respite from the deep winter's cold.

Alberta's namesake, Louise Caroline Alberta, appears to have had as resilient a character as the provincial bloom. The fourth daughter of Queen Victoria had chosen not to marry European royalty, as was expected of her, but instead chose the adventurous Scot, the Marquis of Lorne. He became the Governor General of Canada and in 1881 embarked on a tour of western Canada. He followed the railway to its end at Portage la Prairie, Manitoba, then set of by wagon to see the Northwest Territories. So enthusiastic was he as he toured the land, that he romantically proposed to create a province which he could name for his princess. The following year the Government agreed and rearranged the borders of the three existing districts of the Northwest Territories to add a fourth – Alberta. In 1905 Alberta became a province of the great Dominion of Canada.

Before The Dawn

Long before history could begin its humble tracings ... long before even the first primitive hunters would set foot upon it ... the land that would be known as Alberta was reverberating with the thunderous movements of earth, wind, torrent and fire.

Seventy to eighty million years ago, parts of southeastern Alberta would have been described as a tropical paradise; a low, marshy, humid area dotted with sub-tropical lakes, deltas and streams and covered with lush vegetation. Inhabiting these prehistoric everglades were giant primordial creatures that engaged in a daily struggle for food and supremacy, not only with each other but with the very forces of nature. Both the dinosaurs and their surroundings were victims of an erratic natural history, with frequent floods following devastating downpours. The land was carpeted with volcanic ash which rained from sources as far away as Washington State and southern British Columbia. The earth was in a stage of total transition.

In this wild and primitive area familiar species such as turtles, crocodiles, sharks and salamanders existed side by side with the long necked Plesiosaurs and Mosasaurs, which often measured as much as ten metres (33 feet) long. The mighty, two-ton Albertosaurus (Alberta Lizard), cousin of the fearful Tyrannosaurus Rex, stalked the land, ravaging smaller herbivores. The four-ton Daspletosaurus (frightful lizard), another relative of the Albertosaurus, was a deadly foe, most likely one of the most savage carnivores to be encountered in an equally savage land. Often the only defence against its razor-like teeth and overpowering strength was agility, as characterized by the smaller, swifter flesh-eaters such as the Stenonychosaurus (narrow-claw lizard) and Dromiceiomimus (emu mimic).

For ten million years scores of dinosaur species foraged and fought for existence in this area, before, mysteriously, the entire species vanished into history, leaving an abundance of rich fossil finds in their wake. There are many theories as to why this catastrophe took place, from a supernova or asteroid hitting the earth to a plague which devastated the dinosaurs. More probable is the theory that slow climatic changes over a period of several thousand years resulted in a succession of winters which touched the critical point in the dinosaurs' survival abilities. The mature creatures were unable to hibernate and had no insulation to keep out the cold, while their incubating eggs would have been vulnerable to the extreme temperature changes. Had nature not contrived to leave its footprint in the form of their fossilized remains, many of these mighty creatures would have been hidden from our knowledge forever.

It was the retreat of the Classical Wisconsin Glacier, which covered most of Western Canada some 60,000 to 100,000 years ago, that provided the circumstances for the unique exposure of these prehistoric creatures' remains. At that time, the area on the northern extremity of the great Bearpaw Sea was relatively flat. As the ice sheet retreated, it wiped out traces of previously smaller glacial systems, gouging out great crevices in the flat land. The meltwater channels carved out the land further, draining off to the southeast. Further erosion occurred as rivers and streams constantly changed direction and resulted in this area becoming a catch-all for the debris of that lost prehistoric world. The carcasses were caught in back eddies and sandbanks, then covered in sand and silt from the river banks. The bones gradually absorbed the abundant calcium, silica and carbon and began the slow process of fossilization. Sixty thousand years later, those secrets are now being revealed in what has become known as Alberta's Dinosaur Provincial Park.

Today, Dinosaur Provincial Park is comprised of 8,900 hectares (22,000 acres) of some of the most fascinating country in the world. The valley of the dinosaurs erupts as an astonishing contrast to the great expanse of Alberta grassland that precedes it, dropping suddenly to reveal the bizarre, barren lowland area cut by the curving Red Deer River valley. The valley is broken by an astonishing canyon comprised of bedrock cliffs which offer breathtaking scenery. The river splits the "badlands", so named by the early French traders who travelled through this rugged country because it was of no use for agriculture or grazing. This is the land of the "hoodoo", the strange sandstone rock sculptures revered by the Blackfoot and Cree Indians who believed they had the ability to come to life. And, not least of all, Dinosaur Provincial Park is the site of the world's most important fossil finds, having given up specimens of over thirty different species, with many more yet to be revealed. So important is this site that it has been named as one of UNESCO's World Heritage Sites, an area of "outstanding universal value", along with such international sites as Egypt's Thebes, and America's Yellowstone and Grand Canyon National Parks.

For all the appearance of remote wilderness, the badlands of the Red Deer River Valley support a natural beauty and an undisturbed population of wildlife such as would be hard to find elsewhere. Golden eagles can be seen soaring silently overhead as they seek their prey, returning to their huge nests in the cliffs, safe and protected in the preserve area. Naturalists will also be likely to spot some of the 130 different species of bird life, such as Swainson's hawks, kestrels, merlins and prairie falcons. Great horned owls may also be glimpsed at twilight, as the nocturnal coyotes begin their eerie serenade to the moon. Today the mule deer and the white-tail deer, cottontail and jackrabbits, long-tail weasels, the ubiquitous beaver and timid bobcats all flourish within Dinosaur Provincial Park.

The Nomadic Indians

It is believed that the first inhabitants of Alberta were primitive hunters who roamed its southern prairies following the herds of buffalo. These were the descendants of the first immigrants who, some thirty thousand years ago entered

Alberta from Siberia over the landbridge of what is now the Bering Sea. Over a long period of time they drifted into unexplored valleys and plains, gradually reaching the edge of the glacier. Then the climate softened and the glacier retreated, allowing the nomadic people to move north. Forty-five hundred years ago the prairie Indians arrived in Alberta, and a more complex society began to evolve.

At that time, Alberta's climate was very similar to today's. The few human inhabitants of the northern forests enjoyed a relatively abundant natural habitat, with moose, caribou and deer feeding in the marshes and forested areas, and the clear lakes teeming with fish. In the south, the buffalo also thrived on the prairies and parklands. Their presence bought the prairie Indians in greater numbers and, as their hunting skills increased, so did the population of the tribes. The Indians devised pounds made of logs or brush, and buffalo jumps, where they would drive the herds in great numbers over cliffs to their deaths. With the abundance of food, shelter and clothing provided by the buffalo, the Indians settled on the land and developed a vibrant culture. Social and religious customs developed, and an elaborate ceremonial life followed.

While the northern natives could use the numerous lakes and rivers as their highways throughout their land, the prairie Indians in the south were restricted to walking. They lived in small, self-supporting tribes or families, each occupying its own specific territory, fighting off interlopers or being vanquished as fate would have it. Gradually, four great linguistic tribes emerged: the Athapaskan, Algonkian, Kootenayan and the Sioux. By 1725 their offshoots included the Chipewyan, Slaves and Sekani of the north, the Beaver Indians in the heart of the province, and the Bloods, Piegans and Blackfoot of the prairies south of the North Saskatchewan River. In the east the Crees extended downstream from Edmonton and as far north as Fort McMurray.

The Indians lived with their world as they found it: within their self-made boundaries they were content to live in harmony with nature, if not always with each other. Weaker tribes were absorbed by stronger, and so the established boundaries were always changing. Yet their daily life remained remarkably secure, bound by their communal needs and the shared spirit of the magnificent land in which they lived.

Sadly this life was not to continue. Long before the arrival of the white man in their lands, his presence affected the Indians. Usurped natives on the Atlantic coast began to trek inland, forcing those tribes they met to move on. They in turn pushed those they met further west and the first winds of change were felt. Along with the movement and upheaval caused by their presence thousands of miles away, came the trinkets and tools of the white man: coloured beads, axes and sewing needles, pots and pans. More deadly for the Blackfoot was the "gift" of smallpox – before it was finished it would have wiped out nearly half of the prairie Indian population.

Of great significance to the Indian culture was the arrival of the horse from the south and west and the gun from the north and east. The horse, having arrived with the Spaniards in Mexico, gave them a mobility previously unknown, and the gun, received second hand from the Crees via the fur traders, gave power and protection. The Blackfoot emerged victorious as the prairie tribes battled for supremacy. The golden age of the Blackfoot civilization began.

For nearly a century, beginning about 1775, the Blackfoot culture blossomed. The tribes became much larger as their hunting radius expanded; the horses allowed for longer forays with many more men and consequently larger kills of buffalo. Food was plentiful for all, and with that their leisure time increased. Improved tools, such as knives and files, made life easier and in time helped to produce more new utensils. The women turned their creativity to sewing and decorating, and designed the superbly rich and varied Indian costume which remains a legacy today.

With their horses to ride into battle, the Blackfoot Confederacy, composed of the Blackfoot, Blood and Piegan tribes, became lords of the magnificent Alberta prairies. Their reputation and ability as relentless warriors eventually won them mastery over most of Alberta, Saskatchewan and Montana.

It was in this climate that the Blackfoot flourished and their religion began to take on much greater social and philosophical significance. Great and complicated ceremonies were developed – to celebrate victories, to entice the buffalo, or to honour the sun in solemn majestic tones – giving their deeds and lives greater significance.

Just what would have come from these great beginnings can only be speculated now. The white man's diseases, against which the Indian had little resistance, were beginning to take their toll. The flourishing whiskey trade encouraged a listless, dependent lifestyle. These factors and the growing influx of settlers from the east and Europe, were to make an indelible impact on the evolving Indian civilization, leaving us with only the spirit of this fragile but far-reaching culture to reflect upon.

The New Land

The first white explorer to venture into Alberta was a fur trader by the name of Anthony Henday, an employee of the Hudson's Bay Company. He travelled with a band of friendly Cree Indians and his mission was to "make friends with the natives" and to report back on the nature of the land that he encountered. This was 1784, and Henday's diary described a "level land, few woods and plenty of god water ...". An auspicious beginning for one of Canada's, and now the world's, great farmlands. The Crees led Henday to the Blackfoot, who in twenty years since receiving their first horse were now revelling in the spectacular growth of their culture. Henday was impressed with the Blackfoot and tried to interest them in direct trade for their furs. By now no strangers to the goods of the white man, the Blackfoot declined politely, preferring to deal with the resourceful Crees who had become the entrepreneurial middlemen of the fur trade. Henday learned of the crafty Cree's trade of the white man's goods for furs and pemmican, trade which enabled them to travel swiftly, without stopping to hunt, to the trading posts in Montreal and Hudson's Bay. There was plenty of room for enterprise in this new land!

Soon the Hudson's Bay Company was joined by the North West Company in building trading posts along the great rivers of Alberta, and a period of intense rivalry between the two companies began. These were the days of lusty expansion and raw adventure. Brave men set out from both companies, ostensibly in search of new trading territory, but more often caught up with the heady spirit of discovery. Ultimately the friction between these two great companies led to their amalgamation under the name of the Hudson's Bay Company in 1821, but not before three oustanding men had explored, mapped and opened up nearly a quarter of our North American continent. Today the names of David Thompson, Simon Fraser and Alexander Mackenzie are as familiar as signposts to most

Canadians. Each will be remembered for his own spectacular contribution: Thompson, not only for the immense amount of land survey carried out, but for traversing every inch of the Columbia River; Fraser, for following the river that now bears his name from its headwaters to its mouth; Mackenzie for exploring down the Arctic and up the Peace River to its beginnings, as well as for making the second crossing of the continent, in Canada, not long after the Lewis and Clark expedition had crossed the United States.

Over the next forty years, under the direction of Sir George Simpson, the Hudson's Bay Company helped shape the growth of the new land. Gradually order began to come to the "wild west". The golden days of the fur trading empire were already numbered as the missionaries, miners and homesteaders began to trickle into Alberta.

Drawn by a Christian fervour to save the Indians' souls, the missionaries were among the first non-traders to face the wild western frontier. They arrived with little conception of the hardships they would encounter, nor with any idea of the vastness of the territory that they would try to minister to. Characterized by the Reverend Robert Rundle, the first to arrive, in 1840, and followed by Father Jean Baptiste Thibault and his successor Father Albert Lacombe, the Methodists and Roman Catholics drew together a vast parish of whites, Metis, Crees, Piegans and eventually even the aloof and independent Blackfoot. In order to establish their missions, these extraordinary men travelled thousands of miles by canoe and portage, or tramped on foot behind dog teams, facing starvation and even death in their quest to bring salvation to the west. More than once their leather moccasins or clothing was used as food to tide them over until some nourishment could be found. Their persistence and dedication sowed the seeds that became the foundation of the many religious communities in Alberta today.

Ending the whiskey trade was the first mandate of the North West Mounted Police, the brand new professional cavalry recruited by the government of the new Dominion of Canada in 1870. The Hudson's Bay Company had just surrendered its rights under a royal charter for fifteen million dollars and a thousand acres around each post and the "great lone land" stood alone and lawless. The N.W.M.P. motto, "*Maintains le droit* – Maintain the right" set the tone for a mission more far reaching than just law enforcement. In many cases they became judge, jury and court as they tried to restore dignity to the Indians who were being swindled and impoverished by the unscrupulous whiskey traders. Their role enlarged. As they travelled across the country, the mounted policemen established forts which became the sites of many communities to follow. Of these, Fort MacLeod was one that became a great centre of activity. It was here that their military band first instigated the musical ride, still performed to international acclaim by today's Royal Canadian Mounted Police. The recruits also put down roots, settling on land which they were granted after five years of service. The North West Mounted Police bought a previously unknown idealism to the wild country.

The rush to settle the west came hand in hand with the building of the Canadian Pacific Railway across the prairies and mountains to the Pacific coast. But neither homesteader nor engineer could make their mark until the gangs of land surveyors had criss-crossed the country, marking up parcels and subdividing mile after rugged mile. Not even the famous American "Pony Express" could claim superiority over these hardy crews who braved the extremes of the elements, working inch by inch over wild country and water, laying lines on the lone land that was now to be part of Canada.

The tales of good humour and hardship told by and about these hardy characters bears testimony to the mettle of such early sons of the Canadian west.

At the same time, the first successful attempts at commercial ranching were being made in the chinook belt of the foothills of Alberta, heralding one of the most unique and romantic eras in this province's history. The combined effects of the American cowboy culture on dress, animal husbandry, and even speech, found a happy marriage with the British sense of tradition and gracious living, creating a genteel western ranching style which still lingers today.

By 1883 the railway builders had reached Alberta, and the ring of their sledges reverberated across the prairies. By the end of the century the Canadian Pacific Railway had laid a thousand miles of track in the province, each mile a victory for painstaking physical labour. Now the homesteaders literally began to pour onto the prairies, with colonist trains leaving Montreal and Toronto once a week for the new West.

Growth of the Cities

Alberta is a land of striking contrasts. Towering mountains rise in the west, forming a backdrop to the endless prairies that stretch as far as the eye can see. The rural charm of the wild West coexists with the cosmopolitan chic of its modern cities. While some things have remained the same for centuries, others have changed and grown so quickly as to defy definition.

Alberta's cities, characterized by its two major metropolises, Edmonton and Calgary, have come a long way in a very short time. Both had their beginnings as forts established by the North West Mounted Police in 1875, where they served as meeting places for commercial trade and a focus for the activity of the north and south of the province, respectively. Other cities which have grown from the early pioneer settlements include Fort Macleod, Fort McMurray, Lethbridge, Medicine Hat, Red Deer and Peace River.

Many of the towns and cities were named to commemorate the past, or as nostalgic remembrances of immigrants to countries and people left far behind. Peace River, Red Deer, Manyberries, Pipestone, Smokey River and Seven Persons are translations from the Cree and Blackfoot tongues. Calgary, meaning "clear running water" was named by Colonel Macleod of the N.W.M.P. after his cousin's ancestral estate on a Scottish Island. Banff was named after a town near the birthplace of Lord Strathcona. And many towns were named for the people who helped to found them, such as Lloydminster, named for Reverend George Lloyd, who helped to found a British Community on the Saskatchewan-Alberta border.

Fort Edmonton, located on the banks of the North Saskatchewan River, was named by George Sutherland of the Hudson's Bay Company, as a likely compliment to his clerk, John Pruden, who came from Edmonton, Middlesex, England. The busy fort grew from a fur trading centre to become an agricultural community and then found itself in 1898 to be on the Klondike gold rush route – foreshadowing the days of its present role as a service industry centre. In 1905 it was named the capital city of the newly formed province of Alberta. During the 1920s and 1930s Edmonton's bush pilots became pioneers of the aviation industry, earning Edmonton the nickname "gateway to the north". In 1947, oil was discovered at nearby Leduc and a whole new industrial era began. Edmonton's economic base expanded to accommodate the needs of burgeoning oil, gas and natural resources industry, servicing the area from central and northern Alberta to the Northwest Territories, northern British Columbia and northwestern Saskatchewan.

Today Edmonton has a population of nearly 600,000. Known locally as the Festival City, Edmonton celebrates indoors and out, holding many cultural and arts festivals featuring music, theatre and dance throughout the year. Each July the city indulges in a touch of good natured nostalgia with Klondike Days, a festival which goes all out to relive the 1890s gold rush. The famous Edmonton Oilers of the National Hockey League have kept Edmonton on the sports map with some of the world's best ice hockey, while football enthusiasts have the legendary Edmonton Eskimo's of the Canadian Football league on home ground as well.

Besides sports, Edmonton has a host of recreational attractions, including the exciting Edmonton Space Sciences Centre – the largest planetarium in Canada. It features the GP-85 Cosmorama, the most advanced computer-operated star projector in the world to date, as well as an IMAX, supersized 70mm film format theatre. Another experience awaits the visitor in the form of the West Edmonton Mall, billed as the "Eighth Wonder of the World". An awesome shopping and entertainment centre which covers the equivalent of 48 city blocks, this huge complex includes an NHL size hockey rink, the world's largest indoor water park, an amusement park, golf course and 800 stores. Beyond this, Edmonton boasts the Provincial Museum and Archives of Alberta, Strathcona Sciences Park and the Provincial Legislature Building. The old Fort Edmonton lives on in the park of that name, where the 19th century frontier is re-enacted for the modern day explorer.

Centuries before the N.W.M.P. built Fort Calgary on the banks where the Bow and the Elbow Rivers meet, the site had been regarded as a choice campground by the Indians. Evidently the early traders thought so too, for by 1876 the primitive little outpost had become a thriving commercial centre. Seven years later Calgary was incorporated as a city, by which time it had become the hub of the western wheel of Canada, with the CP Railway running settlers and freight directly to its door. By 1914 oil had been struck near the booming ranching city and land values rocketed. In those heady days of expansion, the climate was ripe for celebration. And celebrate they did, with the first Calgary Stampede – a wild exhibition of the glorious ranching traditions, financed by wealthy and loyal civic supporters and attended by an enthusiastic population well acquainted with the lusty lore of their region. Today this world famous western showpiece is held every summer and continues to draw locals and visitors by the tens of thousands.

Calgary, with a population of over half a million, offers numerous attractions and events, including the permanent Olympic legacies which have remained since the city hosted the 1988 Winter games. One of these is the Olympic Saddledrome, now home to the pride of Calgary's NHL fans – the Calgary Flames. As well as being a head office city and financial centre of the oil and gas industries, Calgary doffs its business hat to put on many others: it is home to the Calgary Zoo and Prehistoric Park, one of North America's best designed zoological parks, as well as Heritage Park, an authentic frontier town. The prominent Glenbow Museum is also situated here, offering a superb historic perspective with its permanent Indian and Inuit art and craft displays, while the Calgary Centennial Planetarium and Science Centre offers a popular, hands-on approach for budding astronomers. The arts are catered for as well as the sciences: the Calgary Centre for the Performing Arts contains one of Canada's finest concert halls and is permanent home to the Calgary Philharmonic Orchestra, as well as to two beautifully appointed theatres.

Resourceful Alberta

Alberta's brief history has been characterized by an innate resourcefulness. The fur traders were the first to capitalize on European fashion trends and brought a healthy trading economy to the new west land. The success of the fur trade attracted others who saw richness in the virgin forests and the timber industry was born. Later it was the discovery of coal and gold that bought opportunity again to Alberta. The beautiful grassy plains that had previously been ignored became home on the range for thousands of headstock, and ranching became the west's newest economy. By the turn of the nineteenth century, agriculture had become the main economy, brought about by the thousands of pioneering settlers who had turned their efforts and energy to the rich soil. By the time Alberta was established as a province of

Canada in 1905, the pioneer society had become of the most dynamic and modern provinces in Canada. Between 1896 and 1913 Alberta attracted a tremendous influx of immigrants, a trend which was to repeat itself again after the two great wars. Then in 1947 a major oil discovery near Leduc ushered Alberta into a new age of progress and prosperity.

Today, Alberta's major natural resources continue to lie in the areas of energy, minerals, agriculture and forestry. The emphasis, however, is on their development through research, diversification and technology. In addition, Alberta's very essence has become a major modern resource, as tourism and recreation capitalizes on some of the most spectacular scenery in the world.

The energy industry has played a vital role in the economic development of Alberta, making a substantial contribution over the last forty years to the province's economy in sales and investment dollars. It has acted as a catalyst for growth in the areas of telecommunications, aerospace and transportation as well as the supply and service industries. The magnitude of Alberta's energy resource base is almost beyond comprehension. Alberta has 77 per cent of Canada's conventional oil, 91 per cent of its natural gas and all of its bitumen and synthetic oil reserves. Synthetic crude is produced from oil sands in northeastern Alberta – the deposits there cover an area the size of the Canadian province of New Brunswick and contain more oil than Saudi Arabia. Alberta is the world's largest producer of sulphur from hydrocarbon sources, while its coal deposits represent a significant source of primary energy and a potential feedstock for synthetic fuels and chemicals. A reliable supply of low cost electricity is ensured with both hydroelectric generation and the abundance of coal and natural gas available in Alberta.

Half of the province of Alberta is covered by forests, an area consisting of some 360,000 square kilometres. While the forestry industry has been a dominant force in the provincial economy, investments in development and the emergence of dynamic new advances in the manufacturing sector ensure that growth will continue into the next decades. The largest development to date will see one of the world's largest single-line pulp and paper mills, built by the Alberta-Pacific Forest Industries. Advances in technology have helped in the development of many special forestry products for world export, creating a strong foundation for an even greater industry growth. A Canadian leader in reforestation standards, Alberta's strength lies in its ability to protect and renew this priceless resource. A forest management policy exists based on the principle of sustained yield, where the amount of timber cut never exceeds the forest growth. Reforestation and regrowth techniques are enforced through regulation and monitoring. Today Alberta's forests are managed for a multitude of uses, not only for the forest products, but for watershed protection, recreation, fish, wildlife and grazing – for the benefit of all Albertans.

The land has always been one of Alberta's great natural resources. Almost 32 million acres (13 million hectares) of cultivated land are used to grow grains, oilseeds, forages and special crops. A further 21 million acres (8.5 hectares) of uncultivated land are used as pasture and forage for livestock. Alberta producers are proud of their worldwide reputation for high quality agricultural products, in particular wheat and dairy and beef cattle. Investment encouraging innovation, research activities and scientific study has resulted in an international reputation in the areas of genetics and embryo transfer, food and beverage processing, increased crop production and efficiency. Alberta remains at the forefront of agricultural innovation, with a total of six Agricultural Research Stations located throughout the province. Three universities and numerous laboratories also undertake research activities which ensure a sustained future growth.

Even before analysts had predicted that tourism would become the world's largest industry by the year 2000, Alberta was well on the way to becoming one of the most desirable leisure destinations in the country. Gifted with the natural lure of the spectacular Rocky Mountains and the highest proportion of park space of any province in Canada, Alberta has put considerable effort and investment into developing many of the other inherently fascinating attractions which lie beyond these vistas. Four world heritage sites, a range of multi-season recreational facilities and a sophisticated hospitality industry will now ensure an even greater attraction. Some say that the most important resource for Alberta's tourism industry is a uniquely human one. The warm western smile has already earned Alberta its reputation for hospitality and friendliness right around the world.

The Majestic Mountains

Six hundred million years ago some of the mightiest mountains in the world were formed at the bottom of a vast, inland sea. As the sea drained, the sea bed, which had been formed by layers of compressed sand, silt, gravel and lime, cracked to form faults. Nearly seventy five million years ago these faultlines in the sedimentary rock broke open, squeezed by enormous forces deep within the earth. Great slabs of rock rose up, folded and buckled, then settled. Canada's great Rocky Mountains were created.

Today the Rockies remain in the same basic shape as when they were formed. One can still see the layers of sediment and occasionally even glimpse the ripple marks made by the waters of lost ages. Fossils of ancient plant and animal life remain encased in its hardened rock. The only changes, beyond erosion, to the shape of the land came with the great ice ages in the past million years. Then the crushing weight of the enormous ice sheets and the slowly moving glaciers deepened the river valleys and gouged out many of the spectacular emerald, turquoise or amethyst coloured lakes that we admire today. The great Columbia Icefield which can be seen at the Southern end of the Jasper National Park is one of the visible remnants of the last ice age, nearly 10,000 years ago.

The Canadian Rockies are the northern segment of a long mountain chain which extends 1200 km (750 miles) from the American border of Alberta and British Columbia to the Liard River Basin, flanked on the west by a distinct trench and on the east by the rolling foothills. The magnificence, majesty and unrelenting beauty of these soaring mountains can leave the viewer breathless: lush mountain meadows dance with a kaleidoscope of wildflowers; the forever-green boreal forests stand silent and undisturbed, preserving a world of perfect natural beauty; milky turquoise glacial rivers twist and tumble down from the high country, carving the virgin valleys as they flow to form new rivers below.

Human settlements have been found in the mountains from as long ago as 10,000 B.C., when Indians lived on the shores of Lake Minnewanka, "Lake of the Water Spirit". However, it was not until the arrival of the railway in 1883 that permanent settlement by the white man began to take place. Not long before that, in 1858, a Dr. James Hector, medical doctor, naturalist and geologist, was the first seriously to undertake any exploration of the difficult mountains to the west. In fact, the Kicking Horse Pass through which the Canadian Pacific Railway took its line across the mountains, was named for an incident in which Dr. Hector's horse kicked him unconscious during his first ascent up the steep channel towards the pass.

Alberta's Rockies include a gift of four spectacular parks: Jasper, Banff, Kananaskis Country and Waterton Lakes National Parks. All four areas offer the modern day explorer tremendous sightseeing opportunities, with each having its own unique attractions. Banff National Park, an hour and a half drive west of Calgary, is located right in the heart of the Rockies. This area was opened up for visitors when the CPR built the castle-like Banff Springs Hotel in 1885. Here one can see the most famous, and many would say the most beautiful, of the lakes in the park – Lake Louise. The lake gleams emerald green against the backdrop of Mount Victoria and its glacier, while its waters reflect the tree covered mountain slopes which surround it. On the shores of the lake stands the lovely Chateau Lake Louise, built on the rocks of the terminal moraine left by the Glacier. Also within the park are the downhill ski resorts of Mount Norquay, Lake Louise and Sunshine Village, all of which offer superb skiing opportunities in spectacular settings.

Established in 1907 as part of the growing National Parks system, Jasper is the second largest park in North America. Its rivers, fed by waters flowing from the Great Divide, all join to form the Athabaska River which flows north into the great Mackenzie River system and thence to the Arctic Ocean. It is the Glacial silt carried down by the streams that gives the Athabaska its characteristic pale green "milky" look. The lakes also often owe their spectacular jewel-like colours to the glacial silt suspended in their waters, characterized by the beautiful Maligne Lake. Between Lake Louise and Jasper lies the Icefields Parkway, 230 km (143 miles) of scenic highway that winds its way along the spine of the Rockies, offering awesome views of the glaciers and the breathtaking Athabaska Waterfalls. Jasper, too, offers fabulous downhill skiing and is known for its beautiful alpine bowls and attractive gladed areas.

Waterton Lakes National Park straddles the Canada/US border and is the world's first international Peace Park. Here, scenic cruise boats offer an excellent way to take in the panoramic views. Kananaskis, lying southeast of Banff and just an hour west of Calgary, came to instant world attention by becoming the site of the 1988 Winter Olympics. Two resorts are located in Kananaskis country: Nakiska at Mount Allan, site of the XV Olympic downhill events, and Fortress Mountain, a full-service ski resort with thirty-five ski runs. This area has been designed to be used as a multi-purpose recreational area, with year round sports activities. Beyond downhill and cross-country skiing in the winter, horseback riding, camping and picnicking facilities provide the means for many people to enjoy the natural beauty of the mountains.

One of the greatest bounties of the majestic mountains is the abundance of plant and wildlife which finds a haven among the broad valleys, forests and meadows. The plants vary greatly, depending on the elevation, ranging from the deciduous trees, mainly poplar and aspen in the valley floors, to the evergreen pines, firs, spruces and the lovely larch, which, unlike the other conifers, turns golden in the autumn and drops its needles. With the exception of the roadsides and riverbanks, the shady forests do not support many flowers. However, above 2,300 metres (7,500 feet), where the trees can no longer grow, lie the wide meadows, flowering with golden arnica, columbine, purple asters, bluebells and splashes of red and yellow Indian paintbrush. Higher still, in the alpine areas, grows an even greater profusion of colour, including the graceful glacier lilies, globeflowers, shining buttercups and dainty alpine forget-me-nots.

Wildlife in the mountains is profuse. A particularly arresting sight is that of the large, dark moose quietly munching on aquatic plants in the marshy areas. Elk and mule deer abound, along with a few caribou. Up high, bighorn sheep and mountain goats meander with great agility, only venturing below the tree line occasionally to supplement their diet with mineral deposit "licks". The famous grizzly bear also tends to stay high, rarely venturing into populated areas, unlike its cousin the smaller black bear, which can be spotted quite often. Coyotes, wolves, cougar and lynx populate the lonely wilderness areas where few people ever wander. Ducks, geese and swans grace many of the lakes and rivers, and overhead the forest rings with the sounds of the jays, magpies, chickadees, warblers, thrushes and the brilliant mountain bluebird.

The mighty eagle lives and hunts in the alpine heights, lending its silent majesty to these magnificent mountain settings.

A Joy for Generations

Nearly 140 years ago, philosopher and writer Henry David Thoreau wrote: "In wilderness is the preservation of the world". Little could he have known just how vital this kind of thinking would be in helping to preserve the increasingly precious corners of the world from the onslaught of "civilization".

In Canada, we have our forefathers to thank for their far reaching wisdom and their efforts to maintain for future generations the unparalleled beauty they beheld in those heady first days of the new nation. In particular, one of the very first men to think in terms of a nature reservation was the great CPR builder, William C. Van Horne. It was his idea to set aside an area of ten square miles around the hot mineral springs of Banff to be held as public property, and the Dominion government agreed. Two years later, in 1887, this area was enlarged to twenty-six square miles. In 1892 another reservation of fifty square miles was established around Lake Louise. The seeds of the great National Parks System were sown.

Today, it is only fair to say that the areas that have survived the waves of explorers, hunters and developers, as well as the buzz of motorized vehicles, have done so because of their status as National Parks. Not only has their natural beauty and the plant and wildlife been preserved, but the rewards from their isolation has been considerable. The virgin forests, managed only by nature, continue to stabilize and purify our atmosphere. Water is conserved and stored within the mountains, then released to the lower areas gradually in spring and summer. All this allows Canadians and visitors from all over the world to experience the true wilderness without taking a toll from the delicate balances of nature.

Alberta enjoys the distinction of containing more national parklands than any other province in Canada. In all there are five National Parks, covering a total of over twenty-four-thousand square miles: Banff (2,564) Elk Island (75) Jasper (4,200) Waterton Lakes (203) and Wood Buffalo (17,300 – including a section inside the Northwest Territories). Both Elk Island and Wood Buffalo National Parks were also set aside as sanctuaries for the preservation of the animals whose names they bear. Information centres, park rangers and naturalists, as well as guides and park museums, are all part of the parks system which enables visitors to make the most of these national treasures.

Alberta also has an extensive system of provincial parks providing a unique complement to its national parks. In all there are over sixty of these parks and wilderness areas situated throughout the province, each representing a particular facet of Alberta's wide and varied landscape. In this way the fathers of Alberta have sought to bequeath to the future generations living samples of their heritage. These parks are comprised of many wild life sanctuaries and wilderness areas: pre-historic sites such as Cypress Hills, Dinosaur Park and Writing-on-Stone near Milk River; others, such as Entrance, near Hinton, Big Hill Springs at Cochrane and Bow Valley near Seebe are valued for their scenic beauty. Alberta was also the first province to establish provincial parks in urban areas. Both Fish Creek Park in Calgary and Capital City Park in Edmonton were designed to give city residents easy access and the opportunity to enjoy these recreational and park facilities.

As well as the national and provincial parks systems, Alberta is home to a number of unique heritage sites, such as the Dinosaur Provincial Park, which UNESCO has recognized as a World Heritage Site. Another fascinating North American Indian Heritage Site, also recognized by UNESCO, is the "Head-Smashed-In" Buffalo Jump located just west of Fort Macleod. This is the largest and best preserved buffalo jump in North America, last used in 1880. Before that, the jump was used for more than 5,600 years by Plains Indians to drive bison to their deaths to obtain food and skins for clothing and shelter. Today, the site can be visited all year round to utilize the fascinating interpretive centre.

The parks offer many exciting ways to experience the splendour of the Rockies: Canadians and visitors alike can be found taking to the trails on horseback excursions that can last as long as a week or more. Climbers have always been challenged by Alberta's lofty peaks and even the mountain-loving amateur, whether climber or hiker, will be lured by the many hikeable routes and well maintained trails to the top. Ice climbing and canyon crawling enthusiasts abound, although many areas operate scenic gondolas and tramways for the less energetic! Summer or winter, sporting activities are always popular: Alpine camping, canoeing, superb fishing and cycling, downhill and cross-country skiing, ice sailing and snowmobiling to name a few. Many resorts offer hot springs, tennis and swimming facilities. Banff Springs is the site of one of the world's top scenic golf courses. Elsewhere the adventurous might like to go heliskiing on the glaciers, or perhaps skirt the ruffled white water on a rafting expedition – the opportunities for sheer physical enjoyment are endless.

For many, the legacy of the national and provincial parks of Alberta lies in the fact that they are there simply to enjoy. For those who care to linger there is also much to learn, for here time stood still. The wildlife, plants and their environment remain relatively untouched by civilization, offering a unique opportunity for reflection, hope and regeneration. History and nature have long been entwined in this country. The parks are there to protect this legacy, providing inspiration and joy for generations to come.

Alberta Today: The People

Even before the first real influx of homesteaders and settlers had arrived at the end of the nineteenth century, Alberta had become home to several small groups of people, including Mormons, Ukrainians and Germans, many of whom had chosen Alberta in their search for freedom from persecution. Some Scandinavians had also arrived via Minnesota and the Dakotas, as well as directly from Europe, eager to break ground and build a future farming in the new land. French colonists had travelled in convoys of covered wagons, coming as habitants from Quebec, immigrants from Belgium and France, and repatriated French, who had previously settled in the United States. These groups settled mainly in the northern woods and forests, where they built their log dwellings. A group of "experienced" pioneers, Anglo-Saxons from Ontario, had also arrived with horses and cattle in search of more fertile land to work. All these early settlers rolled up their sleeves and set to work clearing and breaking the land. In the south, sod was often cut from the virgin prairie to form their first shelters while they set about building frame or log houses. Adding to this colourful blend of early colonists were those of Slavic descent, the Ukrainians who followed the early influences of Dr. Josef Oleskow, who was instrumental in encouraging thousands of his compatriots to settle in the dry prairies of Alberta.

So enthusiastic were the early Ukrainians that in the few years from 1885 to 1910 they succeeded in populating an area of two thousand square miles, from the wooded Saskatchewan valley, over the hills and the glacial gouges, around the Angle, Landon and Rift Lakes. Today Alberta is all the richer for their retained customs and strong cultural presence.

In 1885 the total population of Alberta amounted to some 30,000. Then worldwide conditions conspired to create large scale settlement of Alberta, and one of the most massive immigration stories in North American history took place. Europe and the United States were changing from agricultural economies to industrial societies. This allowed the settlers to farm for profit, not just for sustenance, and created the perfect conditions for specialized trade. New ploughs, binders and other advanced machinery were developed to aid the farmer in large scale farming. More importantly, the newly developed Red Fife wheat proved itself able to withstand the prairie frost. The Canadian Pacific Railway was already in place to transport the wheat across Canada to its British and American destinations. All that remained was the final twist that would open the floodgates and send the eager immigrants in their thousands to the west. This came in the form of enlightened immigration policies on the part of the Canadian government, in particular by Clifford Simpson, newly appointed minister of the interior.

His timing was perfect, tapping as it did the growing favour of the west for immigration as well as the overflow of settlers who had reached the limits of the American west. In two years the population had doubled to 73,000, of which nearly eighty-five percent were rural dwellers. In ten years, by 1906, the rush to populate the cities and work the fertile lands, mines and forests of Alberta resulted in an increase in population to over 185,000. Alberta had come a long way!

Today, Alberta's 2.4 million population comprises a society that has always encouraged the retention of ethnic heritage. For, as settlers struggled for survival in an untamed land, a bond was built which succeeded in uniting their differences and highlighting the individuality and talents of each group. Albertans treasure this inherent diversity and take pleasure in the degree of cohesion, stability and cultural harmony which exists in the province today.

The modern ethnic representation in Alberta today consists, in order of their numbers, of British, German, French, Ukrainian, Dutch and native Aboriginal peoples. Smaller percentages of Chinese, Scandinavian, South Asian, Polish and other groups enjoy residence in Alberta as well.

The unique skills and culture of these people helped to build Alberta. For example, the British and French made fundamental contributions, both historically and culturally, to both the development of Canada and Alberta. Most significant are the judicial and legal systems and the Parliamentary form of government. The Scots were among the first to settle in Fort Edmonton in 1873, and the English and Welsh founded many farming settlements in central and southern Alberta. The Irish made their contributions to farming and the building of the railway. The early Germans were highly successful agriculturalists, whereas more recent immigrants from Germany tended to settle in the area of scientific research. It was French speaking missionaries who founded the first settlement in 1842 and subsequently they established the Grey Nuns and the Sisters of Charity Hospitals in Edmonton and Calgary. The cultural contributions by people of French descent continue to enhance the province today. The rich folklore of the Ukraine, with its dances, theatre, colourful costumes, cookery and intriguing handicrafts are an enduring legacy of those first rural immigrants, continuing even as subsequent immigrants located in cities and towns. Early Dutch settlers arrived between 1904 and 1912 and played a significant role in the development of the agricultural sector. Today they continue to take great pride in their community's culture, maintaining the Calvinist religious traditions that they originally came to Alberta to practice.

The growth of Alberta from a frontier territory into the modern and dynamic province it is today has taken place in a remarkably short period of time. This transformation is testimony to the efforts of generations of Albertans who have made this great western province their home.

The Future: Looking Ahead

It is impossible to look to Alberta's future without giving a moment to the previous generations, whose achievements have provided the foundation for succeeding Albertans to build on. Today the people of Alberta are as diverse as the provinces' original inhabitants, with new citizens living and working side by side with descendants of the pioneers. Whether clearing out a patch of virgin forest to build a humble homestead, or developing the world's largest shopping centre; gambling on the cattle surviving winter, or investing in a new biotechnology pilot plant, Albertans then and now share an uncommon love of their land and the boundless energy and determination to work with the challenges that it provides.

Alberta's population is characterized by a mosaic of backgrounds, religions and ethnic groups. Here the multicultural activities have a rich diversity. Heritage celebrations and programs are well supported and occur throughout the year, helping to maintain and develop these unique traditions for the future. Culturally, Alberta now offers a tremendous choice as artistic, dance, music and theatrical contributions deepen and enrich the provincial profile.

It is not surprising that the old foundations for Alberta's agricultural, trading and energy-based economy should have provided the basis upon which so many new industries continue to be developed; Alberta's forefathers fully appreciated the extraordinary promise of their new land. Today Albertans are using those resources and their considerable talent for innovation to diversify the province's economy. The old frontiers have given way to new. Alberta is meeting the challenges in what is now being called the last real frontier – research and development in advanced technology.

In the agricultural sector, computer controlled irrigation systems and water management programs have transformed the drylands of southern Alberta into productive farmland. Food and beverage processing is now the province's largest manufacturing industry and Alberta continues to pioneer in product development for world markets. As the technological advances continue, tremendous leaps in crop production and farmland inventories have kept pace, establishing Alberta as one of the world's most productive agricultural economies.

Over the past forty years the energy industry has acted as a catalyst for growth in many areas, including telecommunications, aerospace, transportation and supply and service industries. A world scale petrochemical industry has developed, supplying products for use in the pulp and paper, mining, petroleum refining and fertilizer industries. Forest products have catapulted into the future, as specialty products are developed and semi-finished products begin to take their place in the world markets. Advanced technological research and development has resulted in a host of new industries employing laser systems, robotics, even cold climate engineering. Industrial and consumer product manufacturing are also taking their place in Alberta's economic profile. The trading society that began with the furs and flint has come of age.

A look to the future of Alberta brings a positive glow. The spectacular natural wonders which first attracted people to this province now beckon to the world. Increased leisure time and a desire to experience Alberta's kind of wilderness has heralded a new age of tourism and the province has responded to this demand on a sophisticated scale, with many new developments in tourism and recreational facilities, as well as the hospitality industries which serve them. Along with this growth has come a sense of responsibility: the fragile balance of nature must be maintained if Alberta is to remain what she is. Alberta is determined to keep the growth at a level that will not threaten the environment that it so cherishes.

There is still much to learn from the land of the wild rose; its survival through the lost ages has enabled us to discover a tremendous amount about the life that has preceded us and much remains to be revealed. In its short history as Alberta, it has also become the raw material upon which each successive generation will leave its mark. Let us, through our concerted efforts and conscientious management, be the generation that contributed more by taking less. In so doing, we will preserve and protect this magnificent land and ensure a legacy of joy for future generations to celebrate.

Previous page: the Canadian Royal Mounted Police in perfect formation at the Calgary Stampede. The magnificent stump of Crowsnest Mountain (top) guards the north side of famous Crowsnest Pass, which lies on the border with British Columbia. The pass is one of the lowest through the Rockies; settlers moving west preferred to confront the severe weather here rather than attempt a crossing that took them higher up the mountains, even though the wind in the pass sometimes reaches 160 kilometres an hour. Above: the highway south to Waterton Lakes National Park near Pincher Creek at the foothills of the Rockies and (facing page) Pincher Creek environs. Overleaf: strip-farmed fields surrounding the small community of Cowley, where the Rocky Mountains form a dramatic backcloth to simple homes.

Facing page top: students stand guard wearing the uniform of the North West Mounted Police on the parade ground of Fort Macleod near Lethbridge. This fort is a reconstruction of the first fort built by the N.W.M.P. when they moved into southern Alberta in the 1870s. Facing page bottom: the pure white church of Medicine Hat, a town that "was born lucky" according to Rudyard Kipling, since it was built upon huge reserves of gas. Before the present electric lighting was installed, the city's gas-powered street lamps were never turned off; it was cheaper to leave them on. Private companies were excluded from exploiting the gas field; right from the start, in 1883, the town operated its own gas supply. Above: the Bell Tower of Nikka Yuko Centennial Garden in Lethbridge, Alberta's third largest city. The garden is a memorial to the 6,000 Japanese-Canadians who were interned here during World War Two. Overleaf: a Lethbridge wheatfield.

Waterton Lakes National Park (these pages), which lies south of Lethbridge on the border between Canada and Montana, lies the Canadian section of a great international peace park, most of which is in the U.S.A. Established in 1895, the park encompasses both alpine and prairie landscapes – though small, at only 203 square miles, according to one guide it provides "the maximum of scenery in the minimum of space". The park's wildlife is correspondingly varied – a herd of plains buffalo can be seen on the park's northern boundary and grizzlies inhabit the higher ridgetops. Facing page top: the picturesque, chalet-style Prince of Wales Hotel on the banks of Waterton Lake, one of a series of three major lakes in the park named by their discoverer, Thomas Blakiston, in 1858 for the famous eighteenth-century naturalist Charles Waterton. Overleaf: a slight breeze disturbs the perfect reflections in Cameron Lake, which is set in one of the park's loveliest spots.

Facing page top: the arid beauty of the Red Deer Badlands, a long stretch of terrain north of the town of Brooks known as the Valley of the Dinosaurs. Though the area is now parched scrubland, some seventy million years ago it formed part of the lush, swampy shores of a great inland sea and huge dinosaurs roamed the hills. Dinosaur Provincial Park (above and facing page bottom) was formed in 1955 to protect the fossils here, as the site comprises one of the most extensive collections of such remains in the world – indeed, complete dinosaur skeletons have been unearthed here. As a mark of its importance, the park has been selected as one of UNESCO's World Heritage Sites. To guard against damage by the many visitors, part of the area has been designated a restricted zone; so rich in fossils are these rocks, the temptation to remove them is considered likely to be too strong for visitors to resist, and only conducted tours are allowed in the zone.

Top: wind-moulded sandstone rocks in Writing-on-Stone Provincial Park east of Coutts in southeastern Alberta. The park's distinctive name derives from the 300-year-old rock carvings that are to be found on the cliffs here. Since the bedrock that underlies the prairies has been eroded by water and wind into bizarre shapes, such as hoodoos (above), it is believed that the local tribes may have felt that these odd shapes were manifestations of spirits. The petroglyphs incised here were a means of communicating with these spirits and the area was eventually perceived as a supernatural place by the descendants of these Indians. Facing page top: the Red Deer River as it enters Horse Thief Canyon along the Dinosaur Trail (facing page bottom). Overleaf: gullies near Drumheller, a coal-mining town established at the turn of the century.

Right and overleaf: Edmonton, the state capital and the country's most northerly major city. Named for Fort Edmonton, the Hudson Bay Company's trading post built here in the 1790s, Edmonton owes its existence to the mighty North Saskatchewan River as the waterway gave fur traders access to the surrounding countryside. Indeed, so good was the site that the rival North West Company established Fort Augusta nearby in the same decade. Ultimately the two companies amalgamated, but the community was fairly small for its first hundred years until the discovery of gold in the Klondike in 1898. Edmonton was perfectly situated to become a supply base for eager miners, and subsequently grew by leaps and bounds; from 1891 to 1901, the population swelled from 400 to 2,652 and by 1910 it had reached nearly 30,000. Another lucky break, nearer home, occurred in 1947 when oil was struck within twenty-five miles of the city at Leduc. This discovery encouraged industry in the region and today Edmonton is a thriving metropolis of world standing.

Facing page top and top: Edmonton's high-domed Legislative Building, built on the site of the original Fort Edmonton. Constructed of Alberta sandstone and British Columbia granite, the building was begun on November 30, 1909, when the cornerstone was laid by Earl Grey, then Governor-General of Canada, and work was finished by 1912. The dome, with its lantern-like look-out tower, is an excellent point from which to view the city (facing page bottom). Above and overleaf: the Muttart Conservatory and Botanical Garden. Three of the four pyramid-shaped buildings contain a selection of flowers, trees, cactus and other plants, each pyramid illustrating the flora of a particular climate, while the fourth is a show house of ornamental plants that are changed regularly. Still looking *avant garde* today, the conservatory was opened in 1976.

Billed as the "eighth wonder of the world", West Edmonton Mall (these pages) is the largest shopping and entertainment complex in the world and Alberta's premier urban tourist attraction. Even in the heart of the Albertan winter, when the temperature regularly drops below -25°C, tens of thousands of Americans and Canadians brave the arctic conditions of the roads to flock to this spectacular Mall. Here it is possible to wander around in shirt sleeves and view not only some 800 shops, all under one roof, but also fish tanks of bloodthirsty piranhas, gilded cages of brown bears and tropical birds, and pools of performing dolphins and potentially man-eating sharks. Indeed, West Edmonton Mall adds a whole new dimension to shopping.

West Edmonton Mall covers over five million square feet, cost $1.1 billion to build and contains at its centre a five-acre solarium complete with a competition-quality diving pool, a swimming pool (top) with sixteen-foot-high surfing waves and even a beach and palm trees. In contrast to this lush warmth, the Mall also offers a year-round ice rink (facing page). Children can be entertained as their parents shop on amusement rides (above) – among them, one billed as the most terrifying ride ever invented – and on a floating, life-sized replica of Christopher Columbus' Spanish galleon, *Santa Maria* (overleaf). Full-scale sword fights are staged on the deck of the galleon for the benefit of children. The latter are also eager to try trips underwater in one of the centre's four computerized submarines, from whose portholes one can spy shoals of brightly coloured fish, "mermaids" and sharks.

Facing page top: the interior of one of the Muttart Conservatory pyramids, full of succulents and representing an arid climate zone, one of the most unusual sights in Edmonton (overleaf). Remaining pictures: Fort Edmonton Park, dominated by replicas of various buildings of the Hudson Bay Company fur-trading post as they appeared in 1845 and peopled by costumed staff. The most dominant feature of the park is the Big House (above), a four-storey residence with a balcony from which the fort's governor could gain an overview of the day's activities. The fort achieves an authentic atmosphere as even the humblest of buildings have been considered worthy of construction with great attention to detail. Among such are the ice house, in which buffalo meat was stored all year round, the clay bake oven and the public washrooms. The chapel used by the Reverend Rundle, Alberta's first missionary, has also been reconstructed.

Above: a lone pine stands sentinel as the sun sets over Elk Island National Park (these pages) in the Beaver Hills some thirty-two kilometres east of Edmonton. Enclosed by a two-metre-high fence to keep the wildlife population in and intact, this comparatively small park of 194 square kilometres contains North America's largest and smallest mammals, the bison and the pygmy shrew. The park authorities are particularly proud of the fact that one of the world's largest herds of wood bison – an animal once virtually extinct – roams the southern part of this reserve. Animals from this herd have been released in areas that they once inhabited – a fine example of how such protected tracts of land can serve the animal kingdom. Since the fence excludes wolves and other large predators, careful management is required in order to avoid the over-population of the area by deer, or extensive flooding due to the activities of Elk Island's 2,500 beavers, all of whom, of course, are intent upon building dams.

Facing page top: lofty grain elevators – "cathedrals of the plains" – await the trains that will take their contents to market at Ponoka, a small livestock centre first settled in 1881. Ponoka, whose Indian name means "black elk", lies midway between Edmonton and Calgary and, in its agricultural bias, is a typical prairie town. Although agriculture is now quite varied, with crops such as barley, rye, oats, flax, mustard and rapeseed (facing page bottom) being harvested, sixty percent of the land annually seeded to field crops in the western provinces is still seeded to wheat (above). More than twenty million metric tonnes of this grain are produced annually and three quarters of that total is exported. Overleaf: sunset brings a winter's afternoon to a close at Red Deer Lake, which lies close to the small town of Ferintosh, south of Edmonton.

Combines trawl the land at harvest alongside the Trans-Canadian Highway (top), and on the outskirts of Calgary (above) in the shadow of the city's famous Calgary Tower. Such proximity of agriculture to major roads and cities is typical of the landscape of southern Alberta. Facing page: stubble glows sand gold at Pekisko, where cattle ranches (overleaf) and cereal farms share the land at the foot of the Rocky Mountains. Due to the nearness of the mountains, this countryside lies in a rain shadow – the mountains force moisture-laden air moving in from the Pacific to rise, cool and shed rain, so the land here is semi arid. This prompted John Palliser, the leader of a 1857 expedition studying the possibilities for settlement in the area, to conclude that the region was unsuitable for agriculture. Few then appreciated how widespread irrigation of the land would assist cereal cultivation, or foresaw that cattle could thrive on the prairies.

Calgary, Edmonton's keenest rival. Since the Second World War, Calgary, historically associated with the livestock business, has consistently ranked as one of Canada's fastest-growing cities. Just as important as cattle today, though, is the city's transportation role, since it is strategically located on major road, rail and air routes. Major investments in oil and natural gas industries have encouraged phenomenal growth in the past fifty years and, supported by these industries, Calgary has moved from being a mere provincial city to a metropolis of international status. Situated on the Bow River, the city's business section is compressed between the river and the main line of the Canadian Pacific Railway. Seen from the air in the early morning light, the district's skyscrapers seem to promise a bright future for Calgary.

Rising 191 metres above the centre of the city, the distinctive shape of the Calgary Tower dominates the architecture of Calgary (these pages and overleaf), even though other structures now exceed it in height. From the tower a superb view of the surrounding prairies and the distant Rockies may be had. This was once uninterrupted, but now Calgary's burgeoning business district has placed several skyscrapers in the line of view, in particular the sloping Petro-Canada building. The tower also contains a revolving restaurant and is connected with the Glenbow Museum by an enclosed, elevated pedestrian walkway. Such walkways, known as *Plus 15s* in Calgary because they are built fifteen feet above the traffic, have become a feature of Canadian cities in recent years as they provide an excellent means of defying the severe winters, when pavements can be icebound. Top: the stylish slope of the Olympic Saddledome, another Calgary landmark.

Facing page: the central lobby of Calgary's Municipal Building (above and overleaf), a glittering glass and steel construction that is a far cry from the Victorian vagaries of the original pink-roofed City Hall. This was constructed of yellow sandstone, as were a significant number of the city's other buildings following a fire in 1886 that gutted the downtown area. In its aftermath, logs were prohibited as building materials in Calgary and the nickname "Sandstone City" was coined. Today, "Glass and Water City" might be a more appropriate title, since Calgary boasts a superb combination of the two in its new towers and plazas. Olympic Plaza (overleaf) is a fine example of the latter, while one of the most impressive of the former is the huge Petro-Canada Building (top), where a de Havilland Beaver has been hung from a ceiling. De Havilland had considerable success with this aeroplane, especially in Antarctica.

This page: concrete plazas, turfed and decorated with water, provide office workers with a place to relax in during summer lunch times in downtown Calgary. Covering 162 square miles, the largest land area of any city in Canada, Calgary has plenty of room for parks and gardens. These include such as Fish Creek Provincial Park, which is one of the largest urban parks in the world and is located on the city's southern edge, Burns Memorial Gardens and Riley Park (overleaf). Facing page: transit trains and buses have right of way on the city's Seventh Avenue Southwest. Although Calgary has its share of downtown congestion, a three-block pedestrian mall has been created along Stephen Avenue in the heart of the city, enabling a civilized atmosphere of street-level shops, benches and wandering musicians to be created on that human scale associated with a smaller community.

"The Greatest Outdoor Show on Earth", alias the Calgary Exhibition and Stampede (these pages), consumes the city for ten days every July. This is one of the largest rodeos in the world and probably the most famous, with some $500,000 prize money to be won in the West's traditional tests of man against beast: bronc riding, bull riding, steer wrestling and calf roping. Held on the Exhibition Grounds (overleaf) comparatively close to the centre of the city, the Stampede facilities include a 16,000-seat grandstand, a large trade centre, the Stampede Corral ice rink and an agricultural complex. The million visitors who descend on the city to attend the Stampede are entertained by a wide variety of displays, ranging from the Mounties' famous Musical Ride (facing page bottom), square dancing, fireworks (facing page top), Indians in full regalia (above), free flapjack breakfasts at the kerbside and the bizarre spectacle of wild-cow milking!

Above: bareback bronco riding and (facing page top) the technically easier, though potentially more dangerous, saddleback bronco riding at the Calgary Stampede. The addition of stirrups on the latter contest both aids and hinders the rider, since they assist in maintaining balance whilst the horse bucks, but should the rider fall off and his foot remain caught in the stirrup, he risks being dragged. Bull riding (facing page bottom) contains the added excitement –

for the spectators, at least – of the chance of the rider being gored by the steer. Top and overleaf: the fast and furious chuck wagon race, the most famous event in the show. The race has its origins in the impromptu wagon races of cowboys heading home at the end of a round-up. A chuck wagon carried the food – in Western slang, the "chuck". Originally merely a stiff drink and a hot bath awaited the winner; now those first "home" receive prize money in excess of $200,000.

These pages and overleaf: central Calgary by night and in twilight. In the location of head offices, this city can claim third position nationally with fifty-three, a situation that reflects Calgary's status as a world energy and financial centre. Oil and natural gas firms in the city number some 500 now, oil having been first struck in 1914 at Turner Valley, a few kilometres southwest of Calgary. Alberta's first oil refinery opened in Calgary in 1923, subsequent important discoveries at the Turner Valley site established Calgary's pre-eminence in Canada's oil and gas industries, and when vast oil reserves were found at Leduc in 1947, Calgary was ready to exploit them fully. Prior to 1914, the city was a cattle town, southern Alberta's centre for the marketing and transportation of livestock and beef. This cowboy heritage is reflected in the less-than-subtle shape of the Saddledome (facing page bottom), a stadium constructed for the 1988 Winter Olympics.

Top: a winter's day in Banff National Park, as seen from the summit of Sulphur Mountain, a 2.286-metre high peak served by a gondola lift. Sulphur Mountain was so named because of a fault in the rock strata along its base from which seep the hot springs that first brought Banff to prominence. At the base of the mountain, near the gondola lift, lies the Upper Hot Springs pool, where it is still possible to take a steamy, relaxing bath in the sulphurous waters that well up from the depths of the Rockies. The temperature in the pool reaches 33°C and varies little, regardless of the season. Above: sandstone hoodoos cling to a mountainside in Banff National Park, east of Banff, and (facing page) golfers traverse the immaculate lawns of the Lorette fairways on what must be one of Alberta's most beautifully situated golf courses, in Kananaskis, just east of Banff National Park. Overleaf: Nakiska, near Calgary, during the 1988 Winter Olympics.

Late afternoon sun highlights the snows at the head of Bow Valley near Banff in Banff National Park. The great Trans-Canada Highway follows the Bow River through the park, as does the Canadian Pacific railroad. In fact, they are built upon the former course of the river, which strayed from its original path thousands of years ago. As might be expected, this natural corridor through the Rockies is often bustling and noisy now. It was not always so. The route was first used by native people, the Stoney, Cree and Kootenay Indians, who moved on foot, travelling light, in tune with their surroundings. Many years later, at the end of the last century, European miners followed the river into the mountains in search of precious minerals. In contrast with the Indians before them, they came with mule trains and packhorses, loaded down with provisions and equipment. Open meadows at the foot of Mount Eisenhower mark the site of Silver City, a mining town which boomed and died between 1883 and 1885. At its peak, the town could boast a population of several thousand. By comparison, the park today receives over three million visitors a year.

Magnificent scenery surrounds Banff, as is evident in the view from the Park Administrative Building down the town's Main Street (facing page) to Cascade Mountain. Above: guests on the Banff Springs Hotel terrace enjoy alpine sunshine and an unspoiled view of the Bow River as it passes between Tunnel Mountain and Mount Rundle. Tunnel Mountain was so named because the Canadian Pacific Railway Company once believed that they would have to build their railway straight through it – they had, somehow, initially overlooked the broad valley to the north where the line now runs. The Banff Springs Hotel is one of the finest resort hotels in North America. Not long after the Canadian government declared the hot springs area a national park in 1885, the Canadian Pacific Railway Company constructed this hotel on a prime location close by. The hotel has rarely been empty since. Overleaf: snowy veins of the Bow River streak from Banff across Bow Valley.

A cloudy morning in Banff National Park reduces Mount
Rundle to shades of blue. The distinctive shape of this peak,
which extends some ten miles along the edge of Bow Valley, is
geologically described as "dipping layered". One side of it is a
smooth slope from peak to base following the angle of a single
layer of rock; the other is a far more abrupt and dramatic cliff
face, which indicates the point where the mountain was
pushed out of the earth by powerful geological forces a
millenium ago. Overleaf: some of the park's mountains
washed in gold by a winter sunrise. Amid such inspiring
scenery, it is not surprising to learn that Banff boast's one of
North America's foremost schools of visual and performing
arts, the Banff School of Fine Arts, which is part of Calgary's
University of Alberta. In late summer, a week-long Festival of
the Arts is held by the school, giving students of drama, ballet
and music an opportunity to display the talents they have
perfected in this "campus in the clouds".

Above: Second Vermilion Lake provides a mirror image of Mount Rundle in Banff National Park. There are three Vermilion Lakes, all fed by the Bow River (below) and Forty Mile Creek, and surrounded by wetland. Situated just outside Banff, the area is rich in plant and animal life, the conditions being perfect for beaver and muskrat to thrive. Given a truly glorious sunset (overleaf), however, all of Banff's lakes could be christened "vermilion". Peyto Lake (right) is known for its striking colours, especially its intense blue, although it also appears a spectacularly deep green or a bright turquoise depending upon the season. These variations are due to the silt that is carried into it from Peyto Glacier, which is part of the Wapta Icefield. Lying in the centre of the park, Peyto Lake heads the serenely beautiful Mistaya Valley and, thanks largely to its proximity to the Banff-Jasper Highway, is one of the most visited in Banff.

Above: Chateau Lake Louise, a substantial and beautifully situated hotel built beside Lake Louise (below and overleaf) in the 'Twenties. The lake is considered to be the loveliest in the Rockies, and is certainly one of the most frequently visited sites in Banff National Park. A ski resort (left) near the lake ensures that there is plenty to do in winter as well as in summer. Lake Louise was named for a daughter of Queen Victoria, who married the Canadian Governor General in the late nineteenth century. It seems apt, therefore, that the lake has its origins in the Victoria Glacier which lies on Mount Victoria, a high ridge, rather than an individual peak, of ice and snow that dominates one end of the lake. This glacier once stretched to the present site of the Chateau; upon its retreat it left a huge mound of moraine which almost totally dammed the valley, thereby forming the lake.

Facing page top: not yet frozen, the Vermilion River wends its way through snowy spruce and pine towards the castellated face of Castle Mountain (facing page bottom), once briefly known as Mount Eisenhower. According to Indian legend, this distinctive mountain is the home of the Chinook wind, the warm, dry wind responsible for melting prairie snow in spring. Incredibly, the action of this wind can raise temperatures from freezing point to 18°C in a few hours. Top: Bow Lake, which lies some 2,000 metres above sea level and is fed by the mighty Crowfoot Glacier (overleaf). This breathtaking glacier, which seems to cling to a virtually sheer wall of rock, pushes two toes down towards Bow Lake, whose waters combine with others to form the headwaters of the great Bow River in Banff National Park (above).

Top: Banff National Park's Mount Rundle in high summer and (facing page top) after the first snows of autumn. Mount Rundle was named for a Methodist missionary, Robert Rundle, who, on his travels to bring the Gospel to the Indians, passed these ranges in 1844 and saw the mountain that now bears his name. Above: Vermilion Lake in the Bow River Valley near Banff. The Bow River rises at Bow Pass, the highest point on the Icefields Highway in the north of the park. From there it flows nearly 600 kilometres through Banff National Park and beyond to join the South Saskatchewan River. Diverted from its original course by glaciers during the last ice age, the Bow was powerful enough to cut a gap between Tunnel Mountain and Mount Rundle that is clearly visible today. Facing page bottom: Lower Waterfowl Lake in the northwest portion of Banff National Park. Overleaf: the awe-inspiring Ramparts in the Tonquin Valley of Jasper National Park.

Right and overleaf: Maligne Lake, a seemingly inappropriate name for so lovely a stretch of water, one of the jewels of Jasper National Park. This park, the largest in Canada, includes the Athabasca Valley and the surrounding mountains. It was established in 1907 and named for Jasper House, a trading post set up by Jasper Hawes of the North West Company. Today it ranks second only to Banff as a major tourist destination in the Canadian Rockies. Maligne Lake is the largest glacial lake in this part of the Rockies, being seventeen miles long, and lies a mile above sea level. A treacherous ford at the mouth of Maligne River is said to have given a name to it, the canyon, lake and mountain range, *maligne* being the French for wicked. Many fur-traders lost their goods here when attempting to ford a seemingly innocuous part of the river – what they called that stretch is undocumented. It was left to a Jesuit priest, Father de Smet, to record the accepted name in 1846.

Top: the massive face of Mount Robson, at 3,954 metres the highest peak in the Canadian Rockies. Lying in British Columbia, on clear days the peak is visible from the summit known as the Whistlers in Jasper National Park. Above: the town of Jasper, spread out across the wide valley of the Athabasca River, which was once an important fur trade route across the Rockies. Facing page top: the Whirlpool River, which joins the Athabasca south of Jasper, and (facing page bottom) Mount Edith Cavell, named for a British nurse shot during the First World War for helping Allied soldiers to escape from Belgium. Overleaf: Medicine Lake, full in summer in Jasper National Park. For most of the year Medicine Lake is a trickle of water in a gravel bed, but during the summer glacier meltwater fills the bed to eighteen metres in depth. The lake has been likened to a bath without a plug – its waters are continually seeping away into subsurface channels.

Facing page: dramatic Punchbowl Falls, where Mountain Creek is gradually slicing through a forbidding limestone cliff near the town of Pocahontas, and (top) Athabasca Falls, dominated by Mount Fryatt. The falls, some of the finest on the Athabasca River (above and overleaf), drop a spectacular twenty-two metres into a narrow canyon of Precambian quartzite some thirty kilometres from Jasper. The Athabasca – the name derives from the Cree Indian meaning "place where there are reeds" and refers to the river's delta – rises in the Rockies and flows east for 1,230 kilometres to drain into Lake Athabasca. Milky in colour due the suspension of a fine sediment in its waters, the Athabasca is the main river of Jasper National Park and has a glacier, a mountain peak and a pass named for it.

The Columbia Icefield (overleaf), of which the Athabasca Glacier (above and facing page top) is part, is the largest accumulation of ice in the Rockies, stretching for over 300 square kilometres and reaching depths of 900 metres. Meltwater from the icefield feeds rivers that flow into the Atlantic, Pacific and Arctic oceans, indeed, this "mother of rivers" feeds three great systems, the Columbia, the Athabasca and the Saskatchewan. Athabasca Glacier, one of the icefield's nine major glaciers, extends almost to the Icefields Parkway. In its descent it flows over three cliffs, giving it the appearance of coming down stairs. Facing page bottom: Angel Glacier "wings" its way down the face of Mount Edith Cavell in Jasper National Park. For many this glacier resembles the rear view of a hovering kestrel rather more than it does an angel. In such sublime scenery, however, perhaps an angel came more easily to mind to those that christened it.

133

Pyramid Mountain (top), distinctive in its flat-sided symmetry and multi-coloured rock, is one of the best known landmarks around Jasper. The peak's environs, especially Pyramid Lake (facing page) at its foot, are popular sites for picnics. Above: Jasper National Park's Miette River in autumn. The river, which ultimately drains into the Arctic Ocean, was named for an intrepid French explorer, as was Roche Miette, a mountain climbed by Miette, who then sat on the summit and smoked

his pipe, his legs dangling over a fearful abyss. Overleaf: the Athabasca River in winter in Jasper National Park. Perhaps surprisingly, winter in the Athabasca Valley around Jasper is generally pleasant, there being very few days when the temperature drops below freezing. High on the mountain slopes, however, it is a different story; snow still graces the peaks in June and on the Columbia Icefield it is possible to ski all year round.

Right, overleaf and following page: Wood Buffalo National Park, which straddles the Alberta-Northwest Territories border. The park was established in 1922 to protect the last remaining wood buffalo in North America. Then there were a mere 1,200 of them; today they number over 12,000. The world's largest national park, only slightly smaller than Nova Scotia, is also noteworthy for being the world's only natural breeding habitat for the practically extinct whooping crane. The tallest of North American birds, in 1941 there were only fifteen of these magnificent creatures left. Now protected, in forty years they have increased in number to just over a hundred – it is thought that they were never very plentiful, and indiscriminate shooting by man tipped the balance against their survival. Through the southern part of the park flows the Peace River, still following an ancient course - dinosaur tracks have been uncovered along its banks.